Mundi is a series concent[...]
international essays and fiction.

Titles include:

Jan Lobel from Warsaw

Jan Lobel
from Warsaw

Luise Rinser

translated from the German
by Michael Hulse

and
Luise Rinser interviewed
by Michael Hulse

Polygon
EDINBURGH

Original German © S. Fischer Verlag GmbH 1948
Translation © Michael Hulse 1991

First published 1991 by
Polygon
22 George Square, Edinburgh

Set in Linotron Walbaum
by Koinonia, Bury and
printed and bound in
Great Britain by Redwood Press,
Melksham, Wiltshire

British Library Cataloguing in
    Publication Data
Rinser, Luise *1911–*
    Jan Lobel from Warsaw.
    I. Title II. Jan Lobel aus Warschau. *English*
    823.914 [F]

ISBN 0 7486 6074 7

The publisher acknowledges subsidy
from the Scottish Arts Council
towards the publication of this volume.

To my dead friend
Frederick H. Fernbrook

In the autumn of the last year of the war, the mayor of our town in the March came by and told me, 'You'll have to do some work.'

'That's what I am doing,' I said. 'I'm painting.'

He flapped his hand contemptuously. 'You can go along to Olenski's nursery. They've got work for you. Not enough people by a long way.'

Next day I went to the nursery gardens. They were down by the lake, in an extensive acreage with a white house flanked by two old copper beeches, and with long beds and a few green-houses. It all looked rather neglected. A tall, well-built girl was standing in one of the beds, cutting the rotten and limp leaves from heads of red cabbage; the heads were piled in a heap that glistened like tarnished metal. She was working quickly and calmly and the way she stood there, with her tanned healthy skin and thick red hair, reminded me of a powerful, beautiful horse. Now and then, in a pleasantly deep and somewhat rough voice, she called across the beds to the greenhouses, where a lad was picking ripe

1

yellow melons. He was a short, hunched youth with a weather-beaten face. Every time she called he straightened up, said 'yes' in a drawn-out voice that was both morose and cheery, and stared over at her for a good while before he went on working.

The girl was Julia Olenski. I had seen her occasionally in town, wearing a broad-brimmed, bright straw hat and walking in her swaying, carefree way. She was about twenty. People said she was stuck-up and aloof, since she never said more than was absolutely necessary. When she saw me coming she glanced up hastily and brushed back the hair from her brow with the back of her hand and gazed at me coolly. But her eyes were gleaming and moist and hungry for life. I told her why I had come. She nodded towards the hawthorn hedge. 'You will have to ask Frau Olenski,' she said curtly. It perplexed me to hear her refer to her mother as Frau Olenski. The lad looked up at me as I passed: his gaze was sad, like an animal's, and he gave the impression of being a hunchback, though in fact he was only twisted, like a tree-root.

The hawthorn hedge was full with clusters of gleaming berries. I could hear the snipping of shears and the crackle of dried-out greens, and on the off-chance I called out, 'Frau Olenski!' Treading lightly, she stepped round the hedge.

2

She looked like a girl and I could hardly believe she was Julia's mother. Later I discovered that Julia was her step-daughter, from her husband's first marriage. Her ash-blonde hair was escaping from her pinned-up plaits and made a wispy, frizzy frame for her narrow, pale face. It seemed as if some mysterious breeze constantly kept her hair in a state of disorder. This gave her entire appearance a remarkably breezy, fluttery quality. I told her I was supposed to be working for her, and she replied, hesitantly and with sympathy: 'The work isn't easy.' That much I knew.

'When do I start?' I asked.

She pointed to the beds with the glinting shears. The beds were still crammed with late cabbage and beetroots. 'All of that has to be got in before the autumn rain.'

'Fine,' I said. 'I'll be round tomorrow morning.' She wiped her hand on her blue apron and held it out to shake. For a while I watched her gathering the withered phlox stems in her left hand and cutting them with her right. It was impossible to conceive of her as the wife of Karl Olenski, a big bear of a man who was now a captain at the front. Next morning at eight I was back.

The shrivelled-up lad was digging a bed, breaking fat clods of earth into pieces with his spade. Julia was just coming out of the door: she

3

bit into what was left of a sandwich she'd fixed for breakfast, her teeth gleaming, and paused for a few moments in front of the house, looking out across the green lake. Her eyes glittered, and her strong, rested body looked as if it were freshly dewed. But there was unhappiness in her face, as if she was bored by seeing the same things all the time: the nursery beds, flowers, the shrivelled youth, the sedge at the lakeside, the empty expanse of water, and what was left of a landing stage, a few poles sticking out of the water, black and rotten as bad teeth. She yawned and strolled over to the shed where the garden tools were kept. When she saw me she shouted across, provided me with a dozen willow baskets and a sharp knife, and took me to the bed of beets. And there I stood all morning long, pulling the fat, dark-red beets, heavy with juice, out of the ground, and tossing them onto a heap.

After an hour or so, Frau Olenski came by, armed with her big garden shears. 'Don't bend like that,' she said, 'or your back'll hurt tonight.' Her voice was friendly, but her narrow eyes looked beyond me, as if she were alone in the world. Then, with a light, swift tread, she went behind the hawthorn hedge.

From time to time I heard Julia's call, and the youth's drawn-out 'yes'; I could hear Frau Olenski's shears eating their way through the

4

dried-up flower stems; I heard the wings of migrating birds beating at some invisible height in the blue air above me, and I heard the grinding squeak of violet and yellow beet-leaves beneath my flashing knife-blade. Working there was good. But when I was sitting at the lunch table with the others, in the huge kitchen, I felt as if I was in a foreign country. They said not a word, and ate as if they were all alone. Every attempt I made to start a conversation was met with a tired silence. They no longer knew how to talk.

And so the weeks went by and we lived side by side without getting any closer. Nothing improved when, at the end of October, Frau Olenski's twelve-year-old boy returned home from his boarding-school, which had been bombed one night. Thomas was a good-looking, dark, reticent boy, and most of the time he walked about on his own or covered all the paper he could find with drawings he showed to no one.

By November the beds had been turned, the winter lettuces in the fields had been covered with spruce twigs, and the potatoes had been clamped, and there was no more work for me. I no longer needed to go. But if I had imagined it would be good for me to be quite free again, I was wrong. I missed the fresh air, I missed the strong smell of rich soil and the penetrating scent of herbs and plants hung in the shed to dry, and I missed those silent people, strong, tanned Julia, tender, breezy Frau Olenski, dark, roaming Thomas, and even the morose youth with his sad animal eyes. Often I passed the high fence that separated the nursery from the street. But the gardens were bare and deserted. Then snow fell and the long cold set in, and I worried about the winter lettuce, the spinach, and the bulbs and tubers that could freeze or smother or be eaten by mice. I thought of Frau Olenski, who would be sitting at the window gazing across the frozen grey lake, and of Julia, muffled in an old sheepskin, chopping wood to be rid of her surplus energy.

At the beginning of March, Thomas came round with greetings from Frau Olenski, and asked if I could come again: greenhouse work had started. Thomas took a quick, eager look round my studio, let out a sigh of sorts, and disappeared.

The nursery was clear of snow but some of the paths were under water and the earth was shining with wet. Things already smelled of ferment and life. Julia was scrabbling with her strong, dexterous fingers among the boxed plants in the greenhouse, and her eager tongue showed between her gleaming teeth. Frau Olenski showed me how to transplant tender young plants, and her frizzy hair shivered. Franz, who could turn his hand to anything, was replacing one of the roofing panes of glass that had been broken by the weight of snow. They took me in as if I had never been away. But they were even more silent than before. Often it was so quiet when we were working that we could hear the waves breaking on the lakeshore.

One evening Frau Olenski asked if I would like to move into her house. She had two spare rooms that she needed to rent out. One of them was meant for her mother-in-law, the other for me. A few days later I had moved in with the Olenskis, and soon we were joined by the mother-in-law, a semi-paralysed ice-grey woman with deep tear-bags under her misty, owlish eyes. Now the house was filled with people, but they were scarcely to be heard. In the evenings, though, when Julia sang in her room, which was next to mine, the whole house was assailed by a sense of unease that was hard to account for. Frau Olenski walked to and fro in her room with her birdlike tread. Thomas hurried out of doors when twilight fell and vanished beyond the willows and sedge. Franz squatted behind the shed, grey, and so motionless that in the dark I was once about to put down a basket on him, thinking he was a tree-stump.

In the last week of March the south wind

started. The lake made a loud murmuring sound, and tiles flew off the shed roof. And then came the night that changed everything in the house. The moon was full, and it was a bright night stirred by a wild, whistling wind. I was about to go to bed when there was a knock at my door. It was Julia. Her hair was dishevelled like a wild mane.'Come on,' she whispered. 'Something's up.' Impatiently she dragged me to her room and shoved me to the window. A procession of people were moving along the street past the nursery. Slowly and painfully they were tramping by in straggly rows of four, like a herd of exhausted animals. The moon shone bright on smooth-cropped heads and grey-and-white striped, loose clothing. We pressed our noses to the cold pane.

Suddenly a shot was fired, and a second, and a third. The shooting was taken up, wildly, and was instantly at an end. And the people were gone, swallowed up by blue drifts of ground-mist. It was quiet again. Julia was trembling like a tree in the wind. The next moment someone ran from the house towards the gate, at first hesitantly and bent low in the sparse shadows of the bare shrubs, then quickly, throwing caution to the wind, clear across the brightly-lit grass.

'Mother,' whispered Julia. Frau Olenski flung the gate open and vanished the other side of the fence. Julia stamped her foot with excitement,

and exclaimed: 'Why must she go taking danger-
ous risks?' I put my hand over her mouth. The
minutes went by. At last Frau Olenski came back,
with a tall, thin man who leaned against her like
a scrawny, snapped tree. She walked slowly with
him, pace by pace, as if she were pushing some
wooden figure along.

Julia cried out: 'I must go and help her. '

'No,' I said, 'don't.'

She gave me a distrusting and contemptuous
look.

'Are you scared?'

'No,' I said, 'or at least not for myself. But is it
any business of ours? If she tells us about it, fine.
But as it is… ' She shrugged and I saw she was in
a rage, and behaving as if she had been given an
electric shock.

When I entered the kitchen early the next
morning to fetch hot water, Frau Olenski already
had a fire going in the stove. Silently she was
cutting the bread for breakfast. Her eyes were
sunken in her unrested grey face. She said noth-
ing. A while later, Thomas put his tousled head
round the door and asked in a sleepy voice: 'What
was all the shooting last night?'

Frau Olenski asked softly: 'You heard the
shooting?'

'Of course I did,' he murmured. 'I heard every-
thing.'

9

'What do you mean, everything?' demanded Frau Olenski quickly.

'The shooting, what else?' said Thomas, yawning, and vanished.

The next few days were peaceful and warm. The storm had subsided. The earth had dried a little. During the daytime we were able to uncover the lettuces and rake up the dead leaves. In the afternoons, Frau Olenski would push her mother-in-law in her wheelchair to a sunny spot. The old woman would sit there, her hands in her lap, gazing away to the distance with her dim owlish eyes, forgotten by life and by death.

With Julia I lifted the glass covers off the early beds so that the cucumbers could get some air. All of a sudden she said in a low voice, 'She isn't breathing a word.' She had never mentioned that night again, but I sensed that she was continually thinking of it. I did not reply, and she said in vexed tones: 'I can't stand it.' Bewildered, I countered: 'Whyever not?' She tore out a handful of weeds. 'He's still in the house.' 'Yes,' I said, as evenly as I could, 'she's helping him recover.' She snorted angrily and went on with her work in silence. After a while she murmured: 'Don't you find it strange that she won't trust us?' She gave me a challenging look.

I shook my head. 'She's protecting us.'

'Come off it,' she said. 'No one would believe

10

we didn't know about it.' She came up close and whispered, 'He isn't ill any more. All she wants is her secret. That's all. But,' and she rummaged in her bag and produced a key, 'she isn't going to be keeping that secret to herself.'

She dropped the key back in the bag and fastened it with a safety pin. I gaped at her, uncomprehending. She went on in a murmur, as if she were talking to herself: 'It's her fault. Why won't she say anything? No one could stand this.' She turned to me abruptly and said defiantly: 'Isn't that so?' Confused, I replied: 'But what are you going to do? Throw him out? Where is he supposed to go, these days?' She patted her bag with the flat of her hand. 'That,' she said softly, 'is the key to the room where she hides him. She's been looking for it since this morning. She doesn't dare have a new one made.' She gave me a triumphant look. 'Sooner or later she'll have to ask who's got the key, won't she?'

'You don't mean to starve him out?' I was horrified and in my alarm grabbed her arm. She shook me off. 'No one starves that fast.'

In a resolute voice I said: 'No, Julia, you can't do that. It's wicked.'

'Yes,' she said, 'I know.' And she gave me a sad glance and muttered: 'I don't understand it myself.' Then she hurried off and left me to do the work on my own, till Franz appeared at last and

11

helped me, morosely silent. Once again I was amazed at the strength of this little, shrivelled lad who didn't even come up to my shoulder. All afternoon I could get nowhere near Julia: she avoided me. When we ate that evening I saw that Frau Olenski's hands were trembling as she doled out the soup. Julia ate next to nothing. Franz glanced from one to the other, sidelong and apprehensive, and spilt a good spoonful of soup on the tablecloth.

That evening Julia went on singing louder and longer than usual, but then abruptly broke off in the middle of a song, and instantly the house fell silent.

I slept badly that night. Once I thought the door of my room creaked. But who could it be? I fell asleep again. A little later I woke once more, and this time I saw someone sitting in the chair by the window. The profile was clear against the moonlit pane. It was Julia.

'What's up?' I asked, dopy with sleep. She tried to answer, but found it so hard that she only groaned softly. At last she replied in a low, hoarse voice: 'Now I know everything.'

I said nothing, and she went on: 'Yes, I went to see him.' She sat there motionless, hands in her lap, not looking at me, never once turning her head. She spoke as if to herself, relentlessly going on, at times so softly I could hardly hear her, stubbornly possessed of the need to explain herself to me, and understand herself.

'I didn't do it right away,' she said. 'I stayed standing on the cellar steps for a long time. But there was no sense in waiting. I knew I would do it. So I unlocked the door and went in.'

She hesitated, then went on rapidly: 'He was lying there in the bed. With a bandage round his head – at first I couldn't see anything else. Then I said, "Aren't you aware that you're putting us all in danger?" Don't think for a moment he replied. Not at all. Not a single word. He just looked at me. Do you know what he looks like? A bird. Like a bird with a long neck and beak. That's just how he looks at you, too, quite alien. So I asked him again what he thought he was up to, bringing death to our door. When I said that he simply smiled. Just smiled. Then he said, "You're not afraid." He said, "Please sit down." So I sat down, quite mechanically and obediently. I don't think I understand any more why I did that. Do you understand why?'

'Yes,' I answered, but already she was continuing: 'He wasn't remotely surprised to see me. He said, "I already know you." No, I thought, that's impossible, he doesn't know what he's saying, and I was afraid.' Now scarcely audible, she whispered: 'I saw his eyes. Eyes like this… You can't stop looking at them.' For a few seconds she

13

remained totally absorbed in her own thoughts, and then, still whispering, went on: 'He said, "I know you. You sing every evening. All day I wait to hear you sing." "Nonsense," I said, "it's not that good, and my voice is hoarse." "No," he said...' She hesitated. Then, quickly and embarrassed, she said: 'He told me, "You have a voice like a wild dove."' She gave a short laugh. 'It's odd when someone talks like that, isn't it? And with a strange accent too. "Is that so?" I said. "Like a wild dove? Have you ever heard them singing? They squawk and coo and God knows what, but they don't sing." But he only smiled. It annoyed me. All of it annoyed me, do you understand? So I asked him right out, "Why aren't we supposed to know that you are here?" I was expecting him to be nervous. But not at all. He has a way of looking at you and saying nothing. "Well," I said, "I think I know why." And then I really should have gone.'

Julia fell silent. I saw she was wringing her hands more tightly than ever. Then she continued: 'But I asked him, "Why did you turn up here wearing prisoner's clothing?" I knew the answer, of course. I didn't need to ask. But I wanted to hear him tell me. Do you see – I wanted to torment him. And I was tormenting him. I could see. But then he just said it. The way he said it! I've never heard a voice like that. "I am a Jew. A Polish Jew." That was what he said. Just like that. Very simply.'

I could hear from the catch in her throat that she was close to tears, but suddenly she went on hastily and with abrupt passion: 'So I went and got him something to eat, and told him I'd taken the key. He didn't ask why. Just smiled.'

All at once she turned to me and demanded roughly: 'Why did I do all that? Can you understand why?' Vehemently, consumed with the desire to understand completely, she went on: 'I shouldn't have done it. It was a nasty thing to do, if you look at it from one point of view. But if you look at it differently there was nothing else I could do. When I saw him that night, down in the garden, I had such a strange feeling.' She broke off, stood up, pressed her forehead against the window, and whispered: 'Can it be that we have to do things although we don't want to? It could cost you your life – but you still have to do it. Do things really happen like that or am I imagining it?'

'Yes,' I said, 'I've no doubt things do happen that way. They call it fate. But perhaps it's something quite different. I don't know.' She gave me a sad look, as if she thought I had not understood. There was a moist gleam of perspiration on her brow, brought on by talking at unusual length about difficult matters. Slowly she shook her head. 'I don't know either,' she said. 'Why are we made that way?'

Then she went. At the door she turned once

15

more and whispered: 'But if they find out that we have one of them hidden away here, and if they ask me if I knew, I'll tell them, "Yes, I knew, and I went in there to him."' There was a note of triumph in her voice.

Spring had now arrived, and we had plenty of work: digging, sowing, and planting in the fields. Franz went on working like some reliable old engine, driven on by indestructible strength. But Julia was no longer the way she had been in the autumn. At times she went at her work so the earth scattered. But then she would suddenly stand still and stare out across the lake with a lost look until Franz cleared his throat. Thomas was always out in the marsh-grasses somewhere. He had fixed up an old boat and regularly went out on the lake, and generally he brought back a few fish that he would scale and fry himself. Frau Olenski kept house for all of us. She was paler than ever, and had got in the habit of listening to things fearfully with her head cocked on one side. Franz kept a constant eye on Julia, like a watchful dog, but his gaze could not reach her, any more than my words and all the things I wanted to tell her could. So I said nothing.

It grew harder and harder for her. Holy Week came, a week of warm, peaceful days. We picked violets to sell when the dew was still on them, until late into the morning. The beds were vast and crammed, bursting with the scent, and our hands bore the fragrance of violets for days.

One morning Julia said: 'I wish it were over at last.' I said: 'The war won't last much longer. A few weeks more and it will all be over.'

She shook her head slowly, dropped the violets she was holding and looked across the lake, where a strip of morning mist still lingered. At length she picked up the scattered flowers, moving in the tired way of a sick animal. When Franz had gone to the greenhouse she said out loud and quite out of the blue: 'I wish father would come home.' 'Yes,' I said. She gave me her distrustful look, and remained silent.

That evening as we ate she suddenly enquired: 'When the war's over, do they release prisoners right away, or what?' Her eyes challenged all of us round the table. For a few moments there was utter silence. Then Frau Olenski said placidly: 'I don't believe they do. Maybe some will be sent straight home, but not all.'

'Right!' shouted Thomas. 'I know – after the First World War some didn't come home for five years, like Uncle Peter.'

'That's right,' said Julia, in a loud, coarse tone. 'And there were women who had married again in the mean time, and then their first husbands

17

came home.'

'Oh?' called Thomas, all curiosity. 'So then they had two husbands. Funny.'

Abruptly Franz opened his crooked brown mouth and laughed out loud. 'And then they sent one of them packing.' He nearly choked laughing. It was the first time he had spoken a whole sentence at table, and everyone stared at him in consternation. Suddenly he broke off laughing, cast a startled squint about him, and chewed hurriedly. In the renewed quiet the old woman declared in clear tones: 'My son will be coming home again.'

None of us had supposed she ever followed a conversation. Her misty, owlish eyes rested briefly on her daughter-in-law, then sank down once more within. We said nothing else and quickly finished our meal. As she stood up, Julia gave me a significant look, as if to say, see, I was right.

That evening I regretted having moved to the nursery. I felt as if I'd been caught in some grey and dripping fishing-net, and the sensation was unbearably confining. In the late twilight I ran down to the lakeshore and washed in the cold water until my skin burned. But that did not help either.

As I was entering the house, someone came running from the gate. In the half-light, at a distance, the figure looked like a short willow trunk, moving and with flailing branches. It was Franz. He was out of breath. 'They're coming. They're already in town.'

'Who? The Americans?'

'No, no. The Waffen-SS. A squad of the SS.' He took my arm in his hand, which felt like hot wood. 'Listen!'

The wind bore a muddle of noises across. I tried to stay calm. 'They'll just be passing through, that's all.'

Mutely he shook my arm, and his eyes stared into mine. Then he vanished into the dark.

When I turned to go into the house, Julia was standing on the threshold. In the dim light from the hall she cast a shadow like a wolf's. 'What now?' she said calmly, almost coldly. She did not move. I pushed past her. She stopped me. 'What are you doing?' she asked. 'Let things take their course.' She was speaking loudly enough for everyone in the house to hear her. Her voice was hoarse and hard. We eyed each other up like enemies. Suddenly she said in a weary voice: 'Then at least this would all be over.'

At this I grew angry, and I thumped her arm that blocked my way. I did not pause to see her response.

Frau Olenski was standing by the open kitchen window. 'What's going on?' she asked. Her hair was trembling. 'It's very noisy in town today.' She gazed at me helplessly. 'Or am I just imagining it?'

'No,' I told her, 'you're right. Some troops or other are passing through.'

She stared with wide-open eyes. 'Does that ... does that mean the war's moving here?'

'No, not the war.' I was sorry for her. 'But they may quarter soldiers in houses here.'

She came a step closer. 'Do you think they will come here too? We're right out of town, after all.' I felt even sorrier for her. 'We had better expect them here within the hour,' I told her. She shrunk back in horror.

'If need be,' I remarked, pretending to say it in passing, 'one can hide in the coal cellar under the big hothouse.'

'True,' she said hesitantly, and I could see her struggling to overcome her fear. 'It's wrong to be afraid,' she added softly, 'it only brings bad luck.' She smiled, and I left her and went to look for Julia.

It was a deep violet dusk that refused to turn to night. The air was filled with voices and sounds. Cautiously I called out for Julia. No reply. I searched the entire acreage but could find her nowhere. Maybe she had long since gone to her room. Frau Olenski approached, one of her blonde plaits tumbling half-loosed over her shoulder. 'Where is Julia?' she cried out, in so great a despair that she was wringing her hands.

'Julia,' I said, so calmly that it sounded forced, 'will be somewhere in the garden, I imagine.'

'She mustn't!' cried Frau Olenski. But instantly she regained her self-control. Embarrassed, she said: 'Oh God, I'm so nervous.' She tried in vain to pin the loose plait up.

'She'll come, no doubt.'

As if I had voiced some doubt aloud, she obstinately repeated: 'Of course she'll come.' At that moment I sensed that she came very close to betraying her secret to me. Keeping it left her so unbearably alone. But she said nothing and quickly went back into the house.

I ran out into the garden again. The moon was rising above the lake, and the night was somewhat brighter. A figure was squatting at the landing stage – not Julia. It was Franz, cowering in the damp grass, half concealed in the sedge. He did not move, and sat there like a figure from a nightmare. 'Franz,' I said in an unfriendly tone, 'what are you up to there?' He raised his arm very slowly and stretched it out, and his crooked bony finger stabbed in the air. 'There,' he said, 'out there, over there!'

It sounded like a wild animal hissing and spitting. Far out, barely visible, a boat was making for the bay at the other shore. Both of us stared out across the lake, so quiet and glistening, as if it were frozen.

21

Suddenly Franz tugged at my skirt and said in a wheezing whisper:

'Julia and him – I've known about it for a long time.'

I tore free, but he grabbed my dress again and held it tight. 'And you've known too,' he said.

'Don't talk such rubbish,' I said angrily. 'I don't know what you mean. But if you're talking about something you think is meant to be a secret, please keep it to yourself.'

He gave a low snarl. 'Did I say I was going to report anyone?'

'Why don't you just do that!' I yelled.

He laughed a feeble and long-drawn laugh, like a dog howling at night. And all at once, somewhere in the grassy marsh, a bittern began its melancholy cry, deep as an organ note. The little boat across the lake disappeared into the shadow of the bay. Franz uttered a helpless, lamenting sound; I felt sorry for him, but I could not help him, and I went.

I had not gone ten paces when someone came running across the sand, and I heard a high, commanding voice: 'Where is my boat? It was you that cast it off, wasn't it? Admit it was you!' The voice was breaking with anger. 'You helped him. Why did you do that?' I heard the sound of a blow, then two voices raised in anger, and then something splashed into the water.

Thomas passed me slowly, without seeing me, his hands in his trouser pockets. 'The bastard,' he whispered, 'the damned bastard!' He spat like a man, and his face was aglow with triumph.

The water was not deep at the landing stage: the youth hauled himself out, but he did not go up to the house. Dripping wet, he remained cowering in the sedge.

After a while I returned to the house, quite worn by all I had seen, and Frau Olenski met me. 'Where is she?'

I shrugged. 'Let's turn in.' Thomas, who was at the window, turned and gave me a strange look.

I suppose none of us slept that night. Towards morning, as day was just breaking, the steps creaked. My door opened quietly. I held my breath. Julia sensed that I was awake. 'He's gone,' she whispered. 'I rowed him across.' In the half-light she looked grey and strained. 'I'm tired,' she murmured.

'Get some sleep, Julia,' I told her. She remained standing, hesitant. Falteringly she asked: 'Can I sleep here?' She dropped down heavily in the armchair by the window and almost immediately fell asleep. A while later, when it was already light, I heard noise out in the street, and vehicles passing. Hurriedly I started to dress. But no one came to the house, and the silence returned. Morning broke, and the first blackbird began to sing. Julia lay in the armchair, pale and rumpled, but the old downcast expression had faded from her face. She looked almost contented, and was breathing evenly and deep. I let her sleep till it was time to go to our work. She woke up instantly and went out without saying more than good morning.

Day after day and night after night we waited for the looters, or for soldiers to be billeted on us, or for a house search. We waited, and said not a word about it. But nothing happened. Julia made no reference to that night. It almost seemed as if she was gradually forgetting.

It was spring, and all day long people were coming to pick up plants. 'Twenty kohlrabi, thirty early cabbage,' and the next week: 'Twenty tomato plants, ten cucumber, ten celery.' For hours Julia and I were stooped over the early beds digging out the tender young plants. Frau Olenski counted them up and sold them. Franz did the planting in our own beds. Thomas was the only one who did nothing. He drifted far out on the water in his boat, sunning himself or drawing.

We said little. Once Julia pointed to the gardens and said with a wrathful melancholy: 'They'll drive their tanks across there.'

'That,' said Thomas, who happened to be there, 'shows how much you know about it. Why would they pick the soft ground by the lake?'

Franz muttered: 'As far as I'm concerned they

can trample the whole lot of it down.'

'What was that?' demanded Frau Olenski.

'Nothing.' He spat into his hand, and went about his digging so that the earth flew.

Julia had grown lean. Her eyes no longer glittered, but there was a new, powerful brightness about her. Every other night she rowed across the lake. I was the only one who knew. She climbed down and up the trellis. At times when we were working she breathed heavily, and a couple of times her eyes fell shut at meals.

'After the war we'll hire three or four hands,' said Frau Olenski. 'And I'll leave,' said Franz. Frau Olenski looked at him in consternation. 'But Franz, no, we can't get by without you,' she complained. 'You can't do that to us, Franz.'

'We'll see about that,' he growled defiantly.

'He won't go,' murmured the old woman, without opening her eyes.

On the first of May we hung a white flag out, and on the second a scattered number of our own soldiers came by and shot holes in the cloth, and we trembled, but the next morning the war was over for us. We stood beneath the flag, looking at the dirty brown bullet-holes. 'Devils,' said Franz. 'Godforsaken devils. Carry on shooting till the very last moment.' He held his head high, and his eyes were gleaming with pride. 'If the master had seen that!'

25

'Fool,' Julia shouted. 'The master! The master's behind barbed wire, with time enough to think what was right, what it all meant.' She gave him such a malevolent glare that he flinched. Frau Olenski raised her eyebrows but said nothing. Thomas, beaming, exclaimed: 'And now I'll be able to get out of here and go to school again.' His mother gave him a sad look and then said to me: 'And I don't suppose you'll be staying either.'

Julia looked at me, shocked and expectant. 'Yes I will,' I answered quickly, 'I'll be staying.' Julia breathed a sigh of relief, and Frau Olenski said: 'It's too good of you...'

'I like it here,' I said. Which was only half true.

Franz's wrinkled face twisted into a grimace. 'There are good times ahead,' he growled, with a despairing sneer. But no one paid any attention.

On the second day of the occupation, one of our town officials handed me a piece of paper which turned out to be a requisition order for our boat. I passed it on to Julia. She turned pale. 'That's impossible,' she said softly.

'They'll come and take it,' I said. She shook her head. 'We'll see about that.' After a while she threw her rake aside. 'I'll be right back,' she said. For as long as she thought she could be seen, she walked slowly, but then she began to run, so the gravel flew. I heard the hard blows of an axe. Then the squeak of an iron chain. The crunch of the lakeshore sand. When she returned she said: 'Right! I'd like to see them take that.'

'Have you broken it up?' I asked in astonishment.

She gave a short, soft laugh, made no reply, and went on working, almost cheerfully.

Shortly before midday, Thomas came running up. 'My boat,' he panted. 'Who did it?'

'Not so loud, you idiot,' said Julia, and she showed him the commandant's order. He looked at us uncomprehendingly. Julia said: 'Think it out for yourself. Which would you rather have, a couple of boards missing so you can't go rowing for the time being, or them take it away from us for good?'

'What do you mean, us?' he demanded crossly. 'It's my boat. If anyone's going to smash it up it'll be me. Have you got that?'

Julia teased a stone out of the bed and tossed it on the path. 'I can't think where all these stones come from,' she muttered.

Thomas remained standing there with his legs apart, looking dark and aggressive. 'What business of yours is my boat?' he persisted.

Without straightening up she said, 'This afternoon we have to plant more lettuce. Franz has already dug the patch.'

27

Thomas went off irresolutely. Julia mopped the perspiration from her brow. Once Thomas had vanished behind the hedge she said in a low tone: 'I'll go and fetch him tonight.'

I was alarmed. 'But the boat's a wreck.'

'Nonsense,' she said. 'I just knocked a couple of boards out of the bottom. I'll put them back in.'

'Julia,' I cried out, 'it's dangerous. What if the boat leaks? Or if you're seen out on the water? They have look-outs everywhere.' She gestured with her hand as if she were shooing a fly.

All night long I didn't sleep. The moment I heard a sound I leapt up and leaned out of the window. The night was very quiet. Not so much as a dog barking. The reeds were motionless. The lake was as smooth as a mirror. Midnight came and went. Three o'clock passed, and half past, and a morning breeze began to stir in the reeds. It turned cold. At last the trellis creaked, and soon after my door opened soundlessly. Julia dropped into the armchair. 'He's gone,' she said in an expressionless tone. 'The hut is empty. Everything's gone.'

'Perhaps he's already on his way here,' I suggested. She shrugged. Suddenly she laid her head on the arm-rest and began to cry. She made short, harsh sounds, as if she were trying to keep down a dry cough. I kept perfectly quiet and let her go on weeping.

When my alarm clock went off with a rattle soon after five, I started up: I had fallen asleep. But Julia was still crying. I gave her boric acid lotion and cotton wool to bathe her eyes. 'Don't bother, it really doesn't matter at all,' she said, and went down just as she was. We did not have a light on at breakfast, so no one saw how she looked.

That morning, as we were planting out the third sowing of peas in rows, we heard Thomas swearing down at the lakeside. Julia started. A moment later he came running up. 'My boat's down there and it's wet. Somebody's been out rowing in it.'

'In that smashed-up boat?' Julia laughed out loud.

'Don't you go laughing!' he shouted. 'It's true. The oars are wet, and everything. There are strands of weed on the keel.'

'It must be jinxed,' said Julia. 'Who knows, maybe ghosts can row a boat that has boards missing from its bottom.'

Then Franz, who was at the other end of the bed, chimed in: 'Fitting three boards back in is easy if you really want to use the boat.'

Irritated, Julia snapped: 'You're both crazy. Leave me alone.' Thomas scraped at the dry soil with the toe of his shoe, cast us an angry and confused glance, and went off.

Julia went on working, her teeth ground tight shut. Her eyes were inflamed. Her hands were so restless that she had difficulty dropping the dry peas into the straight grooves in the soil, and they missed time and again. It was a good day for planting and setting. Late in the afternoon a light, warm rain began to fall. Frau Olenski came out of the house and let the rain run down over her face and her outstretched hands. She stood there a long while, looking out across the lake. Julia glanced across at her. I had the feeling that in her puffed-up face there was an expression of scorn or triumph; but it was only for a moment, and I wasn't sure. At that moment I wished fervently that the stranger would never come back.

Life went on, day by day, but in some intangible way it was transformed. Of course there were a few noticeable changes. Now, for example, although times were dangerous, the front door was left unlocked, night after night. Furthermore, Julia left the landing light burning into the small hours, and it could be seen at a considerable distance. And Julia herself was different. She was less haughty, but had grown moody and irritable, and she treated her mother with a kind of pitying superiority.

I grasped how profound the changes were one morning in the second week of May, when Franz came running up, trembling with cold and agita-

tion: 'The cucumbers in the open beds have fro-
zen up.' The damage this loss constituted for the
nursery was great. Frau Olenski listened to him
in a manner that suggested he was boring her.
'Frozen, are they?' she said absently. 'We'll just
have to plant out a new lot.' Julia scarcely even
looked up. Franz gaped at them. 'But we covered
them over so well,' he muttered, bewildered and
guilty. 'I've no idea...'

'Forget it,' said Frau Olenski.

He shifted from one foot to the other and gazed
at the floor. Then he ran out in a hurry. On the
threshold he looked round again, a horrified ex-
pression on his face, as if a ghost were after him.

Suddenly, the old woman spoke up: 'It's time
he came.' She lifted her heavy lids and gave us a
penetrating look. Then her eyelids dropped again
like a curtain.

The cold days passed. Gradually it turned
warm once more. The lilac blossomed and faded.
When the jasmine was in full bloom we had the
first thunderstorm. The thunder crashed twice,
three times, and then a wonderful rain poured
down. The last drop had barely fallen when the
evening light fanned out in mighty beams
through the clouds. The garden was resplendent
with deep, succulent green, and the broken jas-
mine flowers shone like yellow cream. The
shrubs and trees were dripping wet. The light

31

trembled on twigs and the tips of leaves in a thousand droplets.

'Someone's coming,' said Frau Olenski. 'I heard the gate.'

We looked out of the window.

'Whoever's that?' exclaimed Thomas.

The old woman listened, her eyes half closed. 'That's not him,' she murmured. But I was the only one who was listening to her, although complete silence had fallen. Frau Olenski and Julia looked into each other's eyes, two snakes drawn up erect, staring, motionless. There was a profound and sorrowful distress in Frau Olenski's face.

'Look,' shouted Thomas, 'he's standing out there, he daren't ring the bell.'

'You go out,' Frau Olenski said to Julia in a soft, imploring tone. The girl blushed deep red and shook her head. So Frau Olenski took her gently by the arm and they both went out. Thomas and I were still standing at the window. 'Do you know him?' he asked me.

'No,' I answered. Which was the truth but was also untrue. There he stood down below, tall and thin, his head bowed slightly forward, his dark eyes fixed expectantly on the door. His dark hair was wet and stuck to his forehead. His suit was dripping wet. And glittering drops of rain were even clinging to his black stubble. He was carrying a sodden cardboard box in his hand. 'What's he doing out in the storm?' said Thomas in a disapproving voice. It was a long time till we heard the door of the house creak open. The stranger dropped his box. Plainly he needed both hands for his welcome, and the fact that his box had fallen in a puddle didn't bother him at all.

'Do they know him, then?' demanded Thomas.

'It seems so,' I said.

'Ah!' he shouted suddenly, and slapped his forehead.

'What's up?' I asked.

'Nothing,' he murmured ominously, and slunk from the room like a weasel. I heard his creeping step on the stairs. Then I too went up to my room. An hour later we were called to dinner. The table was laid as if for a feast-day. Frau Olenski was running busily to and fro between the stove and the table. Julia sat by the window, silent. He was now wearing dry clothes and had shaved, but there was still something savage about him, though you'd have been hard put to say what it was. Maybe it was his big, restless eyes that gazed into nowhere. Sometimes he would focus both eyes on the tip of his long, hooked nose, though without squinting. Julia had been right to compare him to a bird. An untamed, dreamy bird. When he raised his head and stretched his long neck it was easy to imagine him taking wing and flying off the next moment. His slender hands played nervously with a twig of jasmine. He smiled at Julia one moment and Frau Olenski the next, a brief, light smile, as if he were begging their pardon.

'This is Jan Lobel from Warsaw,' Frau Olenski told me. He smiled at me in his friendly, ill-at-ease manner as well, and I was afraid of blushing. His smile, and his timid, untamed nature, bewildered me.

'He has been meaning to visit us for a long time,' said Frau Olenski, and now it was her turn to blush.

'But I lost my way,' said Jan, in the deep, soft voice of the Slavs. He told us how he had strayed into the marshlands, and was found by fishermen and nourished back to strength. As he spoke he stroked the twig of jasmine carefully, and Julia's eyes watched his hands keenly. Suddenly he raised his head and grew distraught. Loud footsteps could be heard out in the street. The steps passed, and he passed a hand across his forehead.

'My God, Jan,' said Frau Olenski in distress, 'it's all over now. You are a free man, Jan.'

He gave an embarrassed and childlike smile. Julia gazed at his smile in delight, and it reappeared on her own face as if reflected there. She realised as much, and looked down. 'Where are

34

you going, Jan?' inquired Frau Olenski. He had stood up and hurried out. We saw him hastening across the gravel yard, his stride long and his arms swinging. On the grass, he stopped and put his head back. It seemed he was enjoying the pure and gentle air on his face.

'He's thin,' said Frau Olenski in a sympathetic tone. Julia nodded absently. Then suddenly we saw a crooked, doubled-up figure weaving through the bushes. 'That's Franz,' whispered Frau Olenski. 'Why isn't he coming in to eat? And where has Thomas got to?' She hurried around excitedly. 'My God,' she lamented, 'I totally forgot them both.'

'Thomas has a cold,' I said. 'He's upstairs. I'll take his food up.' She agreed to the suggestion. Thomas's door was bolted on the inside and he wasn't answering. I put the plate down outside the door as if it were for a stray dog.

When I returned to the parlour, Jan Lobel was sitting at the table again. Franz was perched there too, small and ominous and ready to leap. Jan had left off playing with the twig of jasmine and Julia had stuck it behind her ear. It gave her a slightly jaunty look; although she wasn't saying anything, you could sense what turbulence there was in her spirits. Again and again, Jan Lobel's eyes wandered to the old woman in the wheel-chair. At last, in a tone of hesitant friendliness, he asked: 'Why are you looking at me like that, Mother?'

'Mother?' she retorted, in that rough voice of hers, and shook her head. Then she gave us a penetrating look and said out loud: 'People like that come and go.' Franz gave a vigorous, approving nod, and then squinted across at us, startled.

'That's right,' Frau Olenski said softly to her mother-in-law. 'Do you want anything else to eat?'

But the old woman shut her heavy eyelids. 'Take me to bed,' she demanded. Frau Olenski wheeled her out. The moment she was gone, Franz slipped out too. I was on the point of going as well, but a look from Julia kept me. I could think of nothing to say. And the two of them were silent too. Their silence was of a special, intense kind, and at first I felt I was involved in it as I might be in a conversation, but then, unequal to the sheer power of the silence, I just sat there as if in a daze. When Frau Olenski returned it was late and Jan was tired. That night I hardly slept. Curiosity, the tension, and a deep and abiding fear kept me awake. But the house was completely silent.

The weeks that followed had a magical quality even for me, though basically it all had nothing to do with me. It was June now. The long grass in the meadow swayed in the breeze. Our vegetables flourished as we had hoped. And the weeds grew too and provided us with ceaseless labours. But we managed the extra work faster and more easily than ever. The clear bright weather of early summer had a lot to do with it, but there was something else as well, something that can be described but not really explained. There were a number of strange surprises. Thus one day, for instance, we beheld Jan Lobel pushing the old woman's wheelchair into the shade. She turned her owlish eyes upon him and asked sternly: 'Why don't you go back to your wife and children?'

He replied in a friendly tone: 'I don't have any children.'

Stubbornly, she persisted: 'What about a wife?'

He dug the toecap of his shoe into the grass: 'She's dead.'

The old woman's round, veiled eyes remained fixed on him, unmoving, and she pursued her interrogation: 'When did she die? What was wrong with her?' He did not answer immediately. She waited in silence, alert. Then, abruptly, he declared in a loud voice: 'She died four years ago, in a camp.'

The old woman reflected for a while, then asked sharply: 'Was she killed?'

Jan nodded. Julia and I exchanged glances.

37

What disturbed us more than Jan's reply was that this ancient woman, who no longer seemed to show any interest in the world about her, knew about these things.

'Is that so,' she said, and her heavy lids fell to. She appeared to have dropped off to sleep, and Jan was about to go, when she said, perfectly distinctly: 'But here you're like a fox in a chicken run.' And then, having said this, she really did fall asleep. She snored, loud as an old clock in a church tower. From that afternoon on, not a day passed when the two of them did not have one of their short, intense talks. If he kept her waiting too long, she would sit with her head stretched forward, listening carefully. And once she finally heard him coming she purred contentedly. She treated him sternly, as if he were a schoolboy. But he was the only soul she deigned to talk to at all. God knows what the two of them were always talking about. Sometimes we caught some of it. One day she asked him: 'What do you live on?'

'I am a guest in this house,' he answered gently. She went on in her insistent way: 'What else do you do? What work do you do?'

Shyly he told her: 'I write poetry and stories.'

She thought this over for quite a while. Then she uttered a brief and enigmatic 'Aha'.

On another occasion she asked him: 'When will you be leaving us?'

As friendly as ever, he responded: 'I don't know.'

'You don't know.' She made a sound that was vaguely like the spitting of a cat. After a time she demanded: 'Which of them is it?'

He stood there pulling leaf after leaf off the branch of a beech tree above him and made no reply, merely smiled. She brought her fist down on the arm-rest of the wheelchair and said angrily: 'I thought as much.' Then she fell asleep. Jan remained standing under the tree, chewing at fresh green leaves. Suddenly the old woman asked in her rasping voice: 'How do you keep the two of them from killing each other?'

He laughed softly. Julia blushed crimson. She bent right down over a bed and did not dare look up.

Jan Lobel had also managed to befriend the untamed and wary Thomas. One day I saw Jan sitting on the shore, his legs crossed beneath him, smoking his pipe. Thomas was crouching beside him. I could not hear what they were saying, or even whether they were talking at all. They sat there for over an hour in the blazing sun. Then Thomas got to his feet and ran up to his room. When he came back he had a bundle of papers hidden away inside his shirt. He lost one of the sheets as he ran, and I found it. It was a drawing, made with a very sharp, hard pencil and looking as if it had been done in silver-point, of reeds and a wild duck in flight. I still have it. How Jan had succeeded in taming the child in so short a time is beyond me.

Only Franz and Jan steadily avoided each other, though I, too, kept from being together with Jan. I did so from the very start, and never gave it a moment's thought. Later I hit upon a reason. It was scarcely more than a vague intuition, an apprehension. One day in July I saw Jan Lobel on the lakeshore. I was alone, hidden in the dense foliage of the beanplants, picking the first green runners. It was an overcast day and just beginning to rain. Jan started to strip. He took his jacket off and hung it on a stout rush by the water's edge. But the rush bent, and the jacket fell into the water. Jan seemed not to notice. He slipped off his shirt and hung it on the same rush, which was upright again. This time it bent more slowly, but presently the shirt fell into the water too. Still he noticed nothing. I wanted to call out to him, but some deep and fearful curiosity stopped my mouth. With leisurely, sleepy movements he hung up every article of clothing he'd been wearing, one after the other. And then, when everything was in the water, he finally saw what had happened. He wiped his brow and stared into the water, staggered. Slowly he fished his clothes out again and hung them carefully on the side of a boat to dry. All of this happened as if in a dream. There was a fluid smoothness in his movements that was both beautiful and eerie and it set my heart pounding. Then, still naked, he climbed into the boat and rowed out, pulling in long strokes, and a grey veil of rain came between us.

That evening, dry and wearing a change of clothes, he was sitting at table again, his usual quiet, friendly self. I did not tell Julia what I had seen. It was my secret.

The following week I saw him only occasionally, and mostly it was in the distance. He and Thomas went rambling in the fields more and more, both of them tanned and blowzy, their pockets filled with paper and pencils. There was a wild happiness in the boy, and if I had been one of the two women I should have hated him. But enchantment lay upon them all. They were bewitched by the heat and colours of midsummer, by a dream. The sight of the lush blossoms in the garden, the dark and dangerous stranger, and the breathless lovers, was stunning and unforgettable.

One day I heard another snatch of a short conversation between Jan and the old woman.

'No,' said Jan, replying to something.

Whereupon the old woman shouted angrily: 'You even want the shirt off his back, do you?'

I expected Jan to laugh, but in some agitation,

in a tone I had never heard him use, he shot back: 'Why do you sit there tormenting me day after day?'

'Fool!' snapped the old woman. 'After every summer comes the autumn. But just you bury your head in the sand.'

Jan made no answer and went quickly down to the lake, looking unaccustomedly grim.

Sometimes Jan came to offer his help. Julia and Frau Olenski would shoo him away, reproaching him eagerly and lovingly. As far as I could see he was now fit enough to help, and if he seemed pale beneath his tan it need not mean he had not yet recovered his strength. Once, feeling exhausted and vexed, I said as much to Julia, and she retorted heatedly: 'However can you expect such a thing after all he's gone through!' Her face said even more clearly than her words: 'Leave us our happiness. Who knows how long it will last. One thing you can be sure of: it won't last long.'

But now I observed with increasing frequency, when we sat at table, that Jan would suddenly stare ahead with a lost expression. On one occasion he took a potato from the dish, but before he could put it on his plate he had forgotten what he was doing. He held it in the air for a long time, and then, snapping out of it, dropped it on the table. Julia blushed and quickly put the potato on his plate. 'Jan's dreaming,' she said by way of excuse.

The rest of us looked away. Jan gave an alarmed, embarrassed smile. At times Frau Olenski gave him an astonished, bewildered look, but she was intent on her happiness and was unwilling to have anything interfere. Julia was more perceptive, and sorrowful.

One day when Jan offered his services in the garden, Julia sent him to the shed to fetch something or other, I forget what. She gave him the key. But he was so long about it that I wondered what the problem was and leant over the hedge to see. He was standing in front of the shed, the key in the palm of his hand, staring into nowhere. Julia stared too. Our eyes met.

'Oh heavens,' she exclaimed. 'I've given him the wrong key.' She ran across to him and gently took the key from his hand. He hunched up his shoulders about his head in an odd way, as if he was cold, and walked off down to the lakeside reeds, taking long strides.

But these little moments were the only disruptions, and in the end I was almost used to them. 'He's nervous, after all the things he's been through,' I told myself, 'that's all.' But the helpless fear in Julia's eyes grew from day to day. It was a fear I found both moving and provocative, and during those weeks I frequently thought: I'll hand in my notice today. But I never did.

Suddenly the weather changed. It turned over-
cast and cool, and then the rain set in. And then at
last the day came when all of us abruptly realised
that it was all over: the summer, the magic, every-
thing that had made us happy and had been so
perfect that for once in our lives we had had the
feeling that no one was cheating or deceiving us.
It was strange that we felt that way, because
basically we were not really happy, or, if we were,
it was a happiness that was distinctly problematic
and had us holding our breath.

One evening I met Thomas on the steps to the
laundry room. He kept in the gloom and tried to
slip past me quickly. His clothes hung about him,
torn and dirty, his nose was bleeding, and he was
out of breath.

'Thomas,' I exclaimed, 'for God's sake, what
happened?'

'Nothing,' he said roughly. 'I got into a fight,
that's all.' I tried to hold him by the sleeve but he
scratched at me like a wild animal. 'What's it got
to do with you?' he muttered defiantly. But sud-
denly he added in an abashed tone: 'You don't
have to tell anyone.' A shudder went through
him, and he crept down the steps, his teeth chat-
tering. Hurriedly I ran upstairs and fetched him
some dry clothes. Tight-lipped, he allowed me to
wash his head wound with arnica tincture and
dress it with plaster.

'Who was it?' I asked in passing.

'I don't know,' he said grimly, without looking at me. I could see I wouldn't get anything else out of him. He took refuge in his room as a fox would take refuge in its earth. I mended his clothes in a hurry and tossed them into the laundry.

At dinner, Frau Olenski asked in surprise: 'Why did you get changed, Thomas?'

'Got into a fight,' he said, and bent low over his plate.

'Oh, lord!' Frau Olenski was vexed. 'I suppose it was you that started it again.'

Greatly interested, but gentle too, Jan Lobel asked: 'What were you fighting over?'

Thomas, chewing, murmured: 'We were just fighting.'

I do not know if anyone else had the feeling that he was hiding something important and bad from us, something that concerned us all. I only remember that Julia was restless and that the conversation died for a while. And I particularly recall Franz raising his head for a moment, like a dog that has picked up a scent, and then withdrawing into himself more than ever. I took a sideways glance across at the old woman in her wheelchair, but she seemed to be asleep.

The next few days were peaceful. The summery weather had returned. The phlox, beaten down by the rain, gave itself a shake and flamed

out anew. We were particularly proud of our
phlox. It was planted out in two rows to the right
and left of the centre path, so that a long, broad
double strip of red, purple, blue and white ran
right down the garden, all the colours mixed. It
was an exciting and gloriously sensual sight, the
flowers huge and growing breast-high. All sum-
mer people had stopped to admire them. And
many of them had come to take a good look and
smell the drowsy, sweet, honeyed fragrance that
was carried far on the breeze. A lot of them
offered a good price for a bunch, but Frau Olenski
didn't sell a single flower, though she could have
used the money to improve the hothouses. Nor
were we permitted to pick them for our own
vases, and we would never have dreamt of doing
so. Quite often during the day one of us might
suddenly breathe ecstatically: 'Take a smell at
that!' Or sigh contentedly: 'The dark purple is the
loveliest of all.' And we all knew instantly what
was meant.

One day Franz came running up so fast he lost
his clogs. 'The foreign gentleman,' he panted
(which was how he insisted on referring to Jan
Lobel), 'is picking the phlox.'

'That's all right,' said Frau Olenski. 'Let him
pick some.' Julia had turned pale. 'The phlox,'
she whispered, staggered.

'Yes, the phlox,' said Frau Olenski irritably. 'I

told him he could pick anything he liked. How was he to know he wasn't to touch the phlox?' Franz shifted from foot to foot, then he shrugged, drew in his head, and trotted off like a whipped dog. Julia stood erect, gazing across at Jan, who was wandering about between the rows of flaming phlox, absorbed, reaching out his long arms into the flowering plants here and there and ripping out whole bunches.

'Roots and all!' she snapped. Julia gave me a contemptuous look.

'We have so much,' said Frau Olenski tranquilly, and she went on with her work. But she was breathing short and heavily. 'The frost will get it soon anyway,' she murmured. Yet her gaze still wandered tormentedly to the centre path. By now, Jan could hardly hold the flowers in his arms. He pressed his face right into them, and walked slowly over to us as if in a dream.

'Jan,' said Frau Olenski, 'you can put the phlox in the water barrel if you like. I'll look out some vases later.'

He gave her a bewildered look. 'Vases? What for?' He raised his armloads of flowers high above the two women and shook them so that the blossoms fell off and came drifting down. He did it with such utter seriousness that it startled us.

'Jan,' said Julia softly, in a tortured tone.

Rapidly, her lips trembling, Frau Olenski an-

47

nounced: 'I've never seen lovelier phlox than this. It really is beautiful this year, isn't it?' Jan went off without a word. Julia bent down low over the bed. Defiantly, as if she needed to contradict someone, Frau Olenski said: 'Why shouldn't he pick it? What are flowers there for, anyway?'

I cast a secret glance after Jan. He was standing on the lakeshore, stripping the flowers off the stalks and scattering them on the water. Then he stared at the bare stalks and dropped them as if they horrified him. He stood there a long time, hands outstretched and fingers splayed, and then he kicked sand and stones over the stalks and walked off quickly.

At dinner, Franz asked sullenly: 'So can we sell the phlox now, or what?'

'No,' said Frau Olenski tersely.

'Ah,' growled Franz bitterly, 'I thought maybe we could. The weather will be changing soon.' He pointed his spoon over his shoulder and out of the window, where a wall of gloomy lavender grey was rising.

Next morning it rained, and a day or so later the phlox flowers had been knocked off and were lying in the puddles along the path, drowned and starting to decay. Ruefully I said to Julia: 'It's true, there's nothing wrong with being wasteful.' She gave me a grateful look.

One evening I was fetching kindling from the

shed. Suddenly I heard Thomas's high-pitched voice: 'What are you doing sitting here? The rain soaked that seat.' I did not know who he was talking to. There was no answer.

Thomas called out: 'Are you asleep?'

And Jan's voice replied: 'No.'

'Why are you sitting there stock-still like that?' persisted Thomas. 'It's raining!'

'Yes.'

'Jan,' shouted Thomas in desperation, 'why won't you talk to me? Are you angry with me?'

'No.'

I heard Thomas stamp on the floor. 'Then say something. Say something. I can't stand it.' His voice sounded hoarse and beseeching: 'I don't have anyone but you, Jan.'

'Go inside,' Jan replied, wearied. 'Let me sit here. I've got a headache.'

'Oh, Mother has tablets,' exclaimed Thomas, relieved. 'I'll get you one.'

Suddenly Jan yelled: 'Well go on, then!' Thomas went off, and I could hear he was trying to stop himself from sobbing.

It rained for a week. When it stopped the autumn had arrived, cool and clear. The weather was evidently good for Jan. He seemed almost cheerful.

One evening Julia had gone into town. It was dark and she had still not returned. I fetched my flashlight and went out to look for her. I didn't have to go far. She was crouched up against the hawthorn hedge, in a quite unusual position, kneeling amongst the thorns, resting her head in her arms like a child crying. I switched off the flashlight and went closer. She didn't move. I touched her shoulder. She was trembling like a sick horse. In a dry, hard voice she said: 'I'm leaving.'

'But what happened?'

She lowered her arms. 'They spat at me,' she said tonelessly. Her voice sounded mechanical, like a litany: 'The boys in town are always on the lookout for me. They're going to smash our windows. They threw muck at me. Today they set a dog on me. "Go on, get the —— " – no, I can't say what they were shouting. It ripped my skirt. The whole street laughed. I just ran and ran. I must get away.'

'Julia,' I said, 'people talk a lot. Gossip like that doesn't last for long. People get used to everything. You just have to prove you're stronger than they are.' I went on talking for a long time, choosing my words urgently, persuasively. I can't remember everything I said. But I grew flushed and hot in the dark, because there I was standing preaching, and nobody had molested *me*, and it was no doing of mine that they hadn't. Julia crouched there motionless, as if she were carved

50

of stone. 'There are such a lot of them,' she whispered, and she started to tremble again. At last I got her to go into the house.

But the very next day there was a fresh disturbance. We were just pulling up the beanplants, with Jan helping, when suddenly a stone came flying over the wall and fell between Jan and Thomas, passing within an ace of Jan's temple. He looked up in astonishment, then picked up the stone and, holding it thoughtfully on the palm of his hand, wondered: 'What's this?'

'It'll be kids,' replied Julia hastily.

Jan looked at us, gave a helpless smile, and dropped the stone. Thomas had vanished, but he promptly reappeared. 'No one in sight,' he said, and he spat. Jan touched his arm briefly and walked off, shrugging his shoulders. I whispered to Julia: 'Does your mother know about all this?' She held her hand conspiratorially to her mouth.

The following day my mail included an anonymous letter. 'We would advise you to leave the house. A well-wisher.'

I burnt the note. It did not anger me; quite the contrary. I did not trouble thinking about the curious feeling it aroused in me. Nor did I have time to, since the day now came which we had all felt approaching.

It was one afternoon not long before All Souls and we had our hands full cutting asters and chrysanthemums for wreaths for the cemetery. We were all outside by the big hothouse. It was one of those very clear days you get quite late in the year when the *föhn* is blowing in the foothills.

The sky was a deep blue. Things that were far off seemed close. The air was warm and filled with birdsong. A greenish gold light lay on the meadows – it might have been March. Jan was helping us, in his way. He was sitting there, tying up a few bunches and then daydreaming. Absentmindedly he crushed a big yellow chrysanthemum and sniffed thoughtfully at the bitter juices of the flower. When the *föhn* blew he felt unwell. Repeatedly he passed a hand across his brow and eyes. Julia stayed close to him, her broad figure hiding him away.

'Look, someone else is coming,' said Thomas in a disgruntled tone. 'I put the NO SALES TODAY sign up, too.'

Frau Olenski said: 'If only people would just come when we're open.' She sighed. 'Franz, run along and tell him...' She broke off. 'What's got into you?'

Franz opened his pinched mouth and tried to speak. But all he could do was swallow, slowly raise his hand, and point to the man, who was fussily closing the gate and was in no hurry to come closer.

'Who is it?' asked Thomas. 'Shall I go and ask him what he wants?' Nobody answered him, and he looked at them in turn, perplexed. They were all standing as if they'd been turned to stone. The man approached the house, taking his time, and put down his big wooden suitcase in front of the door. Then he shaded his eyes with his hand and gazed out across the garden. He stood there like that for quite a time without moving, a tall, broad-shouldered man. Then he let his hand fall heavily and moved off, walking down the middle of the garden. Once or twice he stooped down. Once he ripped out a clump of weed; then he took a handful of soil, rubbed it fine on the palm of his hand and let it run through his fingers; then he pulled up a winter radish that had been overlooked, cleaned it off with his hand, took a bite, and spat it out. He was coming towards us, but not once did he look our way.

'What an odd character,' said Thomas dejectedly.

And Frau Olenski said quietly: 'That's your father, Thomas.'

'It is?' Thomas kicked at the gravel. I tried desperately to think up some reason to get Jan away. But my brain seemed paralysed.

The man came closer, taking each step heavily as if his shoes were clinging to the soil. His head was set squarely between powerful rounded shoulders. And then there he was, in front of us. He rubbed his fist against his stubbly chin, making an audible scratching sound, and said slowly: 'Yes, here I am. You have a lot of work.'

'Yes,' said Julia, 'but everything did well this year.' She wiped her hand on her pinafore and held it out.

'Mm,' murmured Olenski. 'And this is Thomas. He's grown.' Thomas held out his hand shyly, then stooped hastily to pick up a chrysanthemum his mother had dropped. Olenski rubbed his chin again and the stubble made a grinding sound. His fist was huge and dark-haired.

'And Franz,' he said. 'Franz is still here too. Hello, Franz.'

The lad edged nearer. 'Yes, sir, I'm still here.'

Then the man raised his head, abruptly, and looked at his wife. 'Yes, Anna, I'm back,' he said uncertainly. She said not a word by way of reply.

'Well, then,' he said, bowing his head again. 'I won't disturb you.' He picked up a chrysanthemum and, holding it, gave it a close look. 'A new variety, I see. They have ones like this in America, only they're even bigger.' He put the flower back. Without looking up he nodded in Jan's direction: 'Is that him?' Nobody answered. Olenski gave a slow, tight-lipped nod.

'Come inside,' said Frau Olenski, 'I'll cook you

something.'

'I'm not hungry.' He dropped heavily onto the seat. 'Just you go on with your work,' he murmured. So we did. There he sat, his elbows propped on his knees. There wasn't a sound except the clicking of the shears and the squeak that came from the juicy stalks of the flowers we were cutting.

Suddenly Olenski said: 'I arrived yesterday.'

Frau Olenski put down her flowers and said: 'I'll make some coffee.'

'No need,' he said hoarsely.

'Don't you want to see your mother?' she asked. 'She's living with us. She's almost blind now and she can hardly move.'

'Later,' he murmured. 'I heard you grew artichokes?'

'That's right,' said Franz, 'we gave it a try. But they didn't grow very big. It's not worth the effort.'

'Ah,' said Olenski. 'I heard about it in town.'

'Come inside,' repeated Frau Olenski. He shook his head. 'You needn't be afraid,' he said. 'It's turned out how I'd been expecting it to. You were always waiting for something like this, Anna.' There was no bitterness in his voice, and very nearly no expression at all. Then he looked across at Jan: 'Is it true that he's a Yid?'

'Yes,' said Julia loudly. 'It's true. And Polish. He was in a camp for six years, Father. They killed his wife.' She looked at her father with passionate defiance. He waved his hand dismissively. 'I don't need to know.'

Just then Jan stood up and approached them. Olenski bowed his head. Jan stopped in front of him, and Olenski looked up at him wryly. 'I ought to kill you,' he muttered.

Jan leant forward slightly. Olenski raised his fist slowly and rubbed his scratchy chin. 'But don't worry,' he murmured, 'I won't do it.'

Jan sat down beside him. 'No,' he said, 'you won't. Why should you? We've both been away from home for a long time.' Olenski gave him an unsure look. For a while they were silent. Then Jan said: 'You've come home.'

Olenski opened up his fist, slowly, and let his long arms hang down. 'Home,' he murmured bitterly.

'Yes, home,' Jan persisted. 'It's your house, your garden.' Olenski neatly caught a fly in mid-flight and crushed it between his fingers. 'You'll go on working here as before. Nobody's forcing you to leave,' Jan went on. Olenski tossed the fly away.

'It's your *Vaterland*,' said Jan.

'So what,' muttered Olenski. 'I don't want it.' Jan gave him a look of concern. 'That's right,' shouted Olenski, 'I don't want it.'

Jan shook his head 'You don't know what

you're saying. I don't have anything left at all. And as of today – ' He held out his hands, the empty palms upwards. 'Nothing more, nothing,' he said.

'Well,' muttered Olenski, at a loss. 'It won't always be like that.'

'Yes it will,' said Jan. 'It will.'

Olenski cleared his throat. 'You don't have to leave on my account. I won't chase you off. It doesn't matter one way or the other.'

'But it does,' said Jan mildly. 'It does.'

Olenski gave him a bewildered look.

'There wouldn't be any more gossip in town,' Jan added.

Nobody had been paying any attention to Thomas, but now he shouted out in passionate tones: 'Stay, Jan, stay. If Jan goes, I'm going too.'

Olenski slowly turned to look at him, and his eyes rested on the boy for a long time. Then he said: 'Going, are you? Eh?'

'Yes,' shouted Thomas, fighting back his tears.

'Be quiet,' whispered Julia. 'Be quiet, Thomas.'

'Let him speak,' said Olenski. 'Children tell the truth.'

Thomas shrugged and remained obstinately silent.

'Go on.' Olenski was growing bitter. 'Say it: it would have been better if I'd never come back.'

'Father,' cried Julia, 'don't make it so hard for us. Can't you see how we feel? Everybody thinks we're doing the wrong thing. But ... I don't know, I can't explain it.'

'Never mind,' said Olenski. 'It's happened now. And anyway I'm not talking about you. And she...' He gave a gentle shrug and turned slowly to his wife. She was leaning against the door of the hothouse, her lips bloodshot, her eyes closed. For a while he looked at her with an expression of amazement, almost of curiosity. Then he rubbed his chin with his fist and said: 'Take your time, Anna.'

She opened her eyes and walked away.

'Come on, Franz,' said Olenski, getting to his feet. 'Show me how the hothouses are doing.'

Franz ambled eagerly along beside him, like a dog, and looked up inquisitively at his master.

Jan looked after Olenski and said: 'A pity.'

'What do you mean?' asked Julia, alarmed. He shrugged. 'When you go, Jan,' she said, 'take me with you.'

He smiled at her. 'No,' he said, 'no.'

'But you'll take me,' yelled Thomas, 'won't you, Jan!'

Jan shook his head. 'Where will I be going, anyway?' He looked up and held his finger in the air. 'Which way is the wind blowing?'

'From the south-west,' said Julia. 'Why do you ask?'

'Then I shall head north-east,' he answered

earnestly.

'But Jan,' cried Julia, 'you can't just go if you don't know where.'

He placed his hand on her arm and gazed at her intently. 'Where was I going when I came here?' He gave her a gentle shake. 'See. Let me be. I'm having problems thinking today.'

The sky had clouded over without our noticing. Jan walked slowly down to the lakeshore and vanished amid the reeds.

'Is he going?' whispered Thomas.

Julia went back to her work. 'How would I know,' she muttered. I left her alone and carried the bunches that had already been tied up into the house. I was putting them in the cellar, where it was cold, when I heard Olenski's voice upstairs. He was talking to the old woman. who was sitting on the south side of the house in her wheelchair. I couldn't see either of them, but without intending to I eavesdropped on part of their conversation.

'No,' he said, 'I didn't have it badly.'

I could tell from the creak of the wheelchair that she had suddenly turned to face him. 'Are you going to give her a thrashing?' she asked.

'Why would I do that?' he countered. 'She did the work, she kept the business going as well as she could, she looked after you. Why would I want to thrash her?'

There was a pause, and then she asked: 'Either you're very stupid or very clever. Which is it?'

He gave a sigh, and it sounded like a sigh coming from a deep cave. Then he said: 'How can a woman like that help it?' The gravel crunched beneath his heavy tread. But he stopped once more and said: 'Really, how *can* people help it?' I watched his strong, tired legs pass the cellar window at a ponderous pace.

When I returned to Julia I could tell from the determined movements she was making with her hands and arms that she had reached some definite decision or other. She gave me a blank look but said nothing. As darkness fell and we walked towards the house, she cast long, searching glances into the garden, glances that frightened me.

'Julia,' I said, 'don't do anything hasty. You're not cut out for homelessness.'

She shrugged and was silent. I tried again. 'Men like Jan never stay in one place, Julia.'

To which she simply replied: 'I know.'

She stopped. In the dark I could see her penetrating scrutiny fixed on me. 'If you were in my place, would you let him go like that? Can't you see what a bad way he's in?' There was nothing I could say. She went on: 'I'll get things ready. We can take the night train. Perhaps you'd tell the others tomorrow morning. I'll write later. Stay on a little longer if you can. Mother needs you around.'

Dinner was as quiet as it used to be before Jan came. Everyone's heads were deep down over their plates.

An hour later, all was silent in the house. Olenski paced heavily about the garden, and I did not hear him come back in though I stayed awake late. Shortly before midnight, Julia came in, dressed for travel. 'He's gone,' she said, stunned. 'He hardly took a thing with him. He went just as he came.'

I made a miserable attempt to comfort her and said: 'Maybe he's just outside somewhere?'

'No,' she said, 'he's gone. I know.' And suddenly she gave in to her despair: 'How am I supposed to find him at night?' She wrung her hands.

'Take the bike,' I said. 'You could ride after him.'

She shook her head. 'Which way? And he won't be on the road anyway. I shall never find him again.'

At that moment I experienced a strong feeling of relief. But Julia's pain made me feel ashamed. She stared into nowhere and said: 'I had a cat once, and one night it disappeared. I looked everywhere for it, but I knew from the start that I wouldn't find it again. When I did find it, it was dead.'

'But Julia,' I said, 'you mustn't think like that. He isn't that ill. He'll be heading for a resettlement camp and he'll write some time.'

She gave me a long look. At that moment she was many years older than me. I could see that she understood the full harshness of her loss, entirely. Never again would she meet a man like him.

At breakfast Jan's place was unoccupied. Olenski demanded grimly: 'Where has he got to?'

I answered: 'He's left.'

Olenski muttered: 'I didn't drive him away!' He glanced hastily at his wife. She said calmly: 'What did you expect a man to do?'

He drew his head down, hunching his shoulders, and finished his soup. Franz eyed his master sideways, grief in his crumpled face.

The old woman raised her heavy lids and her owlish eyes swept the table. Then she nodded. 'Men like that come and go.' Her voice sounded vexed as she continued: 'He used to tell me such lovely stories. Now it will be boring again.' Everyone looked at her in concern. She shut her eyes and murmured something we couldn't catch.

Thomas suppressed the sobs that were rising. Olenski got to his feet, put his cap on his head and went out, silently. Franz followed.

Thomas put his bread in his pocket and went too. As Frau Olenski was clearing the table she said to Julia: 'Don't forget to take the flowers to town.'

We fetched the bunches of flowers from the cellar, stood them in tall baskets, and loaded the baskets onto the cart. Julia took hold of my arm. 'Would you go, please? I can't face things today. I just can't.'

Franz stomped like an old nag as he pulled the cart. Halfway he stopped and gave me a miserable look. It was the look of a sad old dog that has been beaten.

'I've been here thirty years,' he said. 'I used to carry her all over the garden when she was small.'

'Oh, Franz,' I said, 'we all have our sorrows.'

He pulled his hat over his face, spat into his hands, and took up the shafts again. But before he went on he asked hesitantly: 'Will she be going now as well?' He waited for my reply bowed as if expecting to be hit.

'No,' I said, 'I don't think so.'

'As long as she doesn't take sick,' he muttered, starting off and hardly audible. He did not intend the words for me.

The townspeople looked at us with curiosity and sympathy. And when we were back we both heaved a sigh of relief.

Thomas was not at lunch. That in itself did not arouse much comment, since he was often late if he took the boat too far out. But that evening he still wasn't back. The boat was hauled up on the shore, dry. As dusk fell we searched the house, garden, lakeshore, and finally the town. One boy remembered seeing him with a rucksack, but he couldn't remember which direction he was going. Early next morning, Olenski notified the police.

Julia said to me: 'Thomas was as good as his word. What about me?' She groaned. None of us did any work or ate a thing that day. Late in the afternoon two policemen brought the lad back. He walked stiffly between them, his head held high. Frau Olenski ran up to embrace him, but he pushed her aside, grim and resolute, like a man.

Olenski said hoarsely: 'So there you are.' Thomas stood in front of him, his gaze challenging. Olenski turned and thrust his hands in his pockets. Thomas went past us, alone, silent, and went into the house.

'Bloody rascal,' laughed one of the policemen. 'He'd already walked forty kilometres.'

'Come in and have a drink,' said Olenski.

That was my last day at the nursery. I moved back to town, and for over a year I couldn't pluck up the courage to visit the Olenskis.

But one day not long after Easter 1947 I went out to the lake at last. From far off I could see that they had built a new hothouse. The whitewashed walls, the brand new wooden beams, and the windows with their gleaming reflections, aroused a disagreeable feeling in me, as if they had been indecent. I strolled along the fence a couple of times before I ventured to open the gate. It was the same garden I knew so well, and yet it was not the same. The hedge had been cut back rigorously, the lakeshore had been cleared of reeds, and the dense shrubs were gone. A few workers I didn't know were digging the perfectly straight beds. Olenski, his cap pushed back, was marking out the paths.

Frau Olenski came to meet me. She had grown older and was very pale. 'Yes, it's all different now,' she said, giving the garden a brief look. 'We only grow vegetables now.'

'It all looks very trim,' I said, 'very nice.'

'Do you like it?' she inquired mildly. Without waiting for an answer, she said: 'Julia is in the little hothouse. Come on in for a coffee afterwards.'

My heart pounded when I saw Julia again. She gave a little cry. She was more beautiful than ever, but there were deep shadows under her eyes. I could see she had done some crying.

We sat on a bench amidst crates of young tomato plants and geranium seedlings. The acrid, bitter-sweet smell of the plants and the rich, wet soil filled the warm, moist air.

'Yes, life's going on here,' she said. 'Plenty of work. Father is in command. We're not doing badly. He bought the plot of land next door. Grandmother? She's totally paralysed now and can't speak at all. Thomas is back at the grammar school.'

There was a forced vehemence in the way she spoke and she hardly let me get a word in. Suddenly she broke off in mid-sentence and pulled a letter out of her blouse. 'There,' she said, 'read that.'

It was a grubby note and the writing was almost illegible. It was dated half a year earlier.

'I found your address in Jan Lobel's pocket. I think you should know that Jan Lobel from Warsaw drowned in August trying to stow away on a ship to Palestine. We buried him in Trieste.'

She put the note away again, saying: 'At least I know that no one's going to throw him out of anywhere again. But you're crying!' She was stunned. 'You're crying over Jan!'

'No,' I said hastily, 'no, I'm crying for everybody who hasn't got a home.' She looked at me closely and then with an expression of deep shock, and I

could see it was no longer necessary to tell her
the truth.

LUISE RINSER
interviewed by Michael Hulse

MH: Could you tell me something about your parents and your relations with them?

LR: It's hard being an only child, and the only child of a father who is a teacher. You have to be a model child, at school and in the community. And I never was. Which upset him greatly. He had an image of how he wanted me to turn out, but it never matched the way I was. My father was very musical, and I owe my musicality to him; he was an extremely good organist. My mother was a very intelligent woman, and I think I inherited some of her powers of understanding. From my father I also got a tendency to melancholy. I was a very lonely child. But perhaps I wouldn't have become a writer if I had had an easier childhood. It was because I had a melancholy, lonely childhood that I started to write very early in life. It was my salvation, and always has been.

MH: But before you took to writing you worked as a teacher, didn't you?

LR: Not at all – I started writing when I was eight! [*Laughing*] I've always written.

MH: I was thinking more of the start as a writer which you describe in *Den Wolf umarmen*[1] [*Embracing the Wolf*].

LR: When I was twenty I wrote a three-part

novel. And a good deal more besides. I burnt
almost all of it. But we're talking about published
books. When I wrote my first book I was twenty-
eight. My fiancé found the manuscript on my
desk and read it. If it hadn't been for him I don't
know if I would ever have become a professional
writer. What he read was the manuscript of my
first book, *Die Gläsernen Ringe* [*The Glass Rings*,
1941]. He said it was really good and I was a
writer, and I told him: You're insanely in love
with me and you've taken leave of your senses.
My fiancé knew a lot about literature and he said:
We're sending this to Suhrkamp Verlag. At that
time Suhrkamp was S. Fischer. They weren't two
separate houses yet. So he forced me to send it
out, and back came the reply from Peter
Suhrkamp: It's marvellous, send us everything
you've got. And I didn't have anything to send
because I'd burnt it all. So he had me go to the
Berlin offices and gave me a talking to, and he
drew up a contract even though the book wasn't
finished yet. I said: Herr Suhrkamp, I'm getting
married and I want to have children and I don't
want to be a writer at all. And he patted my
shoulder and said: You *will* be a writer. You'll
write this book and many more besides. You'll
always be a writer. Then I went home. While I
was expecting my first child I finished the book,
and it had hardly been published but it was

banned. In the Third Reich. It wasn't an anti-Fascist book – you couldn't publish anti-Fascist books inside Germany, I might just as well have put the noose round my own neck – but it was so *un*-Fascist and *un*-nationalistic that it was banned. And that was the end of my career till '45.

MH: The same was true of your career as a teacher, wasn't it? You refused to join the Party.

LR: It was the end of two careers at a single blow.

MH: Two authors to some extent influenced *Die Gläsernen Ringe*. One – whom I know you reject – was Ernst Jünger: you've left an account of how his description of a tiger-lily inspired your own description of the lily in *Die Gläsernen Ringe*. The other was Hesse – who was to praise *Die Gläsernen Ringe*. What meant more to you at that time: Jünger's stylistic approach, or the tone you partly copied from Hesse?

LR: I wouldn't say 'copied'.

MH: Borrowed, perhaps?

LR: No, I'd say our tones harmonized. We have a great deal in common. Not in terms of our generation: he was a lot older than me. But the south German character, the musicality, and a certain leaning towards religion and the Far East – yes, harmony. As for Jünger, I have nothing whatsoever in common with him. Quite the contrary: I cannot stand him. But in those days I was thinking: I have to learn how to write. I didn't know I already could; I thought I had to learn how. And then I saw a copy of Jünger's *Das Abenteuerliche Herz*[2] [*The Adventurous Heart*] and I thought: Ah, *that's* how you write! Not: That's *what* to write. That's *how* to write. The only thing I took from Ernst Jünger was that precise description of a lily. Of course I did something totally different with it.

But the real influences were quite different. My favourite writer is Joseph Conrad. I think I've read everything he wrote. He has always fascinated me.

MH: He must have been a very unusual influence at that time, since Germany is still in the process of 'discovering' Conrad. He still doesn't have the currency one might expect him to have. And it would surprise me to hear that he was widely published during the Third Reich.

LR: I don't mean during the Third Reich. I mean afterwards.

MH: So he influenced the books you published after the War?

LR: Yes. And the first writer to influence the young post-War generation was Hemingway.

MH: Can we stay with Hesse for a moment? Forty years later you wrote in your diary: 'The kitsch elements in Hesse are truer and profounder than the highly artistic elements in Thomas Mann.'

72

Can you explain what you meant?

LR: It's a difficult question to answer. I was thinking specifically of Mann's story 'Die vertauschten Köpfe' – that is to say, of Indian material in the two writers. Thomas Mann did not understand it at all, whereas Hesse had a thorough grasp. At any rate, Hesse – and Thomas Mann too, if I can be permitted an impertinence – both writers have kitschy passages. If I think of *Dr Faustus*, there are scenes where I want to say: If only I could edit these out for you. All the Munich business, which is superfluous given the marvellous rest of the book. Hesse inclined to what one might call kitsch. But then, Thomas Mann – Faustus, I mean – made his pact with the devil, and the devil is cold. Hesse could never have done that, neither as literary artist nor in real life. Hesse was a warm human being, though he did become a sullen old gentleman, true. Thomas Mann became a sullen old gentleman too – but he was *cold*. I've given a great deal of attention to Thomas Mann and his kind of coldness; of course his coldness wasn't entirely genuine – he suffered far too much to be cold through and through. I wrote a piece on 'Hesse and the Far East' for a colloquium in Berlin; it was published by Peter Suhrkamp. And an article on 'Thomas Mann and Socialism'.[3]

Still, neither of them is the writer for me. *My*

writers are people like Joseph Conrad, who is free of kitsch. It's pure. You can look but you won't find any softness in him. Now I've surprised myself: no softness. Apparently I am fascinated by hardness – not human hardness, but the hardness of a substance. Crystal, say. Glass is a substance I love very much indeed.

MH: And Jünger, of course, is not only cold but (as you aptly describe him) necrophiliac.

LR: And Luciferian.

MH: It's tempting to see your origins as a writer as lying in the tension between two opposite poles: the warm-hearted biophiliac Hesse, and Jünger the necrophile.

LR: I think you are over-estimating Jünger's importance for me.

MH: I wouldn't want to over-estimate it; plainly he only played a part in your beginnings. To continue with the War years: you were denounced and sent to prison, and recorded your experiences there in your *Gefängnistagebuch* [*Prison Journal*].[4]

LR: I wrote it while I was in prison. On scraps of paper – newspaper that was meant as toilet paper because we didn't have any other. I wrote it with a stub of pencil I found in the cell. And I was able to preserve the journal, rolled up, and deciphered it after the War. For a long time I wondered if I *ought* to publish it (as I said in my foreword) because I thought: the things I went through – difficult though they were (I was practically starving when I was released, and sick, and humiliated of course) – were nothing compared with the sufferings of those who were in the concentration camps. At heart I was ashamed of writing it down. But on the other hand, prison life in those days... I was expecting a death penalty. It was only a matter of time. The prison was used for detention while a case was being heard, and mine was under way in Berlin at the *Volksgerichtshof*, so it was serious. But I wasn't tortured.

MH: One has the impression that the War years were a formative influence – quite apart from literary influences, which are of secondary interest in this connection. You lost your husband and were left to see two children through on your own. You weren't allowed to practise your profession. And then you were put in prison. Then suddenly you emerged into the ruins, a writer – and a changed, maturer person.

LR: Till then I was more or less a bourgeoise. In fact I'd say that *Die Gläsernen Ringe* is a comfortable middle-class book. Suddenly I was confronted with the toughest reality – my fellow-prisoners were women they called Yankee whores, or thieves and infanticides. Previously I would have looked the other way. And suddenly I began to understand them and love them. It shaped me. And I became what one could call a Socialist, in the widest, deepest sense. People ask me what I am, and I say I'm a Socialist. And they ask what that means, and I reply that Camus once said that Socialism means sleeping on the bare earth till your brother has a bed. That is my definition of Socialism, and in that sense I am a Socialist. And my conversion was a direct result of the time I spent in prison. Some of my family were poor people and some were very rich, and we always had very mixed feelings about possessions and really always inclined to non-ownership. That feeling has survived in me. That's why I did not really suffer from my poverty as such in the Third Reich (and I really was very, very poor) – at least, I didn't suffer much. Almost everybody had nothing. What did cause me suffering was seeing my children go hungry. It was the most difficult thing of all, and the real threat: not knowing what to give the children to eat the next day. Not just my own children. All the children.

So that was how I acquired my interest in the poor in countries that are termed 'Third World' nowadays. I am pleased I was torn out of my bourgeois existence. And I think that if I were to lose everything now, if I had to leave my house and garden, I would say: Very well, I'll take my favourite books with me and my dog and I'll go.

They can't take anything away from me any more. Do you understand? For instance, if I lose things – I inherited some very pretty jewellery from my grandmother, and bit by bit I lost it all, without any great regrets. I blush to admit it, but I wouldn't care to give my car away. I love driving. Still. And I still drive very fast. It's only environmental concern that keeps me from using the car when it isn't necessary. There, that's my confession.

MH: You quoted Camus, and in your diaries you rephrased his statement in your own words: 'Definition of Socialism: To go hungry until children in the Third World no longer die of starvation. To go without inessentials till everyone has the essentials. To be inconsolable till all have been consoled.' It's striking that your brand of Socialism tends to be of an ethical nature rather than economic or political (though those aspects are included too, of course). I always have the feeling that it originates in deep ethical convictions, and is part and parcel with your religious convictions; while the economic and political factors that Marx foregrounded are of secondary importance in your view. Would you go along with this?

LR: Yes. But I have worked in practical politics too. For instance, in the Seventies I did groundwork for Willy Brandt's *Ostpolitik*, speaking in right-wing areas. I wrote leaflets. I joined peace marches and anti-nuclear demonstrations, worked for the Greens, and was even nominated by them for the presidency – with some support from the SPD and FDP. I joined protests against neo-Fascists. And from an early date I often went to East Germany to read and give talks. It was a way of building bridges. I mean to help develop East-West cultural exchanges now. I'm a member of the International Committee for the Reunification of Korea, which to my mind is different from German reunification, which I am no advocate of. Ever since 1947 I have worked for peace and European unity, giving talks and publishing articles, and I've written books on social issues such as equal rights for women. All in all, I've learnt to approach politics realistically.

MH: As you say, your political commitment dates back to the immediate post-War years. At that time you were involved in the 'de-Nazification' process (a process which was left far from complete, indeed hardly even attempted, in many sectors). Could you describe your involvement?

LR: I attempted too much. I went to speak to SS men in a de-Nazification camp near Stuttgart. My subject was 'Hitler within ourselves', and I tried to appeal to the men's conscience, tried to change them. They were all intellectuals. And not long after they all occupied important positions in the Fatherland. That was my experience of it.

MH: Did the terms *Trümmerliteratur* and *Kahlschlag*[5] mean anything to you?

LR: Yes. But, strange though it may sound, I did not bother very much with literature. Not literature as such. Though I reviewed for the *Neue Zeitung* for eight years.

MH: A good deal of what you wrote then is now seen as classical post-War literature, from the short story 'The Ginger Cat' to the novella *Jan Lobel from Warsaw*. So you made your contribution to the attempt to come to terms with, to cope with, the immediate past.

LR: That's true. The subjects I wrote about then were the fate of the Jews, hunger, and then the emancipation of women and prison reform.

MH: Before we started the tape we were talking about the anthology Wolfgang Weyrauch edited in 1949, *Tausend Gramm*. Only three of the thirty writers in it were women, and we were astonished to see that major names of the time, such as Elisabeth Langgässer and Gertrud von le Fort, weren't in it. Of course their approach was radically different; and editors in those days were after their *Kahlschlag* authors. You said just now that a style of writing [*Schreibstil*] adapts to the style of the times [*Zeitstil*]. I wonder if you could describe that need to write utterly differently

79

from the way authors wrote before.

LR: We were all much harder than we had been before. I'd been in Braunschweig and Rostock with the bombs dropping in front of the house and at the back and me with a baby in my arms. If you'd been through the bombing, if you were pleased to get a Care packet from the States after the War, if you even begged, or slept with Americans just for cigarettes if you were a woman so that you could trade them for food for your children – well, things like that change you, whether they concern you directly or you only look on. It was purgatory. All the sentimentality had been stripped away. You've only to think of my story 'The Ginger Cat'. We had been hardened. And we had learnt to endure a great deal. My generation, those who're still alive, are a hard generation really.

MH: But the tone of *Jan Lobel from Warsaw* isn't hard. There's very little of the 'Ginger Cat' hardness in *Jan Lobel*. The mood is even tender, very tender.

LR: Yes; it's veiled. Acted out behind veils, if you were to make a film of it. Of course, you don't always have to be hard. But the core had been hardened. I feel that it's difficult to throw my generation, whereas the youngsters of today break down if things seem to be going wrong in the world. Whereas we say: If we survived *that*, we'll survive this too.

MH: *Jan Lobel* shares a quality with your much later novel *Der schwarze Esel* [*The Black Ass*, 1974]. In both of them we feel that an alternative, obverse side of history is being told, the women's side, the 'passive' side: not 'passive' in a negative sense but rather in the sense that women passively experienced the War because it was forced upon them. The War was started by men and fought by men, and the women were simply there and had to get by as best they could. Was that how you saw it at the time? Was that part of what you wanted to say in *Jan Lobel*?

LR: You absolutely must not ask me what I meant. Whenever people ask about my intentions I give very unfriendly replies. Or: Why do you write? I ask them: Why do you *breathe*? I don't have any intentions. I see things, I see characters. In *Mitte des Lebens* [1950, published in an American translation as *Nina* in 1954 but long out of print] what I heard was a name, Nina. I tried to imagine a woman to go with the name. It's a hard name, a Russian name. And the name took on contour and became Nina. And then Nina acquired a sister, for dialectical reasons. But I didn't have any intentions; she was simply there as well. Nina was a revolutionary, an emancipated woman – and her other self was a bourgeoise. Of course I can analyze myself and see both of them in me.

Mitte des Lebens was the first women's eman-
cipation novel in Germany after the War – and the
men hated it for that reason. I got hate letters
from men, because they identified with Dr Stein,
who is far weaker than Nina. It was a good sign:
those men felt that the book was addressing
them. It disturbed them. I always was an emanci-
pated woman without knowing it, even before the
word was in use. In the book of essays from 1944
to 1967, *An den Frieden glauben*, I've included
pieces that show I knew at an early stage what
women's emancipation means.

MH: Nina is very much on the side of life, to put
it in simple terms. But near the beginning of the
novel there is a striking sentence: 'Her longing
for death is curiosity, a metaphysical curiosity
that originates in her vitality, her audacity, her
urge to know everything – including death – that
she sees as a part of life.'

LR: That is Dr Stein about Nina.

MH: Yes. But I thought I detected the same
tension again, the same as in the two figures of
Hesse and Jünger, the biophiliac and the necro-
philiac poles. In one person.

LR: You can call it by a variety of names. Yin
and Yang, for instance. Nothing is free of these
polarities. For a while, for instance, I was quite
pointlessly preoccupied with the question
whether God was good or evil. If I use the word

God at all now, I don't say he is either good or evil.
He created the world from tensions within him.
There is no such thing as a contented writer, a
contented artist who draws purely upon happi-
ness in his creative work. We are like the frog in
the Chinese tale that falls into a tub of milk and
kicks about in desperation till he suddenly finds
he's churned the milk to butter and has solid
ground beneath his feet. Thomas Mann, for ex-
ample, lived in profound despair. He wrote for his
life. At times when he was uncreative he would
say: Writing my diary is my salvation. He had to
write something or other, no matter what.

MH: You knew Mann slightly, didn't you?

LR: I wrote him an impertinent letter, to which
he replied; I think it was in 1948 – the letter is now
in the Thomas Mann Archive in Zurich. For some
reason I can no longer remember I wrote that he
was a great writer [*Schriftsteller*] but not a great
poet [*Dichter*]. It's a position I could argue now,
even, but it's not necessary. He defended himself.
He wrote me a very angry letter. But we did meet
in pleasant circumstances. I had written an arti-
cle on the suicide of his son Klaus, in the *Welt-
woche* in Zurich, titled 'On the High Wire'.[6] Some
time after I was introduced to him in Munich, and
he said to his wife, or Katja said to him: 'This is
Luise Rinser, who wrote so beautifully about our
poor Klaus.' And a tear ran down his face. I've

never forgotten it. It reconciled me to everything I don't care for in Thomas Mann. One tear. Afterwards I thought: How you have suffered. Some American described him as the saddest child of Fortune in our times. Well put.

MH: In the 1950s you got to know the composer Carl Orff and married him, and a few years later you separated. How did you meet, and what kind of person was Carl Orff?

LR: The way we met was characteristic of him: he took one look at me and fell in love. I looked very young, much younger than I actually was, like a nice, healthy, tanned Bavarian lass – which wasn't what I was, but I looked like it. And Orff saw this girl and thought: This is the one to rescue me from my melancholy. Of course it's deadly if you start a marriage imagining you can save a genius from his depressions. You can't. And two creative people cannot live together. But I don't regret the marriage. He used to play to me. He was composing *Oedipus* at the time. He would work at the piano and I'd be listening, and if I flinched or said *mmm* he would say: No good? It was a very pleasant kind of collaboration. I used to go to rehearsals and premières, and I learnt a great deal in the process. But in the long term it was an impossible marriage.

MH: It was also the period of the Cold War, which was crowned in 1961 with the building of the Berlin Wall. You once wrote that 'the Germans are incapable of objective political thought'. Do you stand by that, following the events earlier this month? The fall of the Wall can, of course, be seen, at least in part, as a consequence of Willy Brandt's *Ostpolitik*, which you supported. How do you see Germany's capacity for political thought now?

LR: Now that East Germany has shown such political maturity, I wouldn't dare to re-assert what I said in general terms. I have tremendous respect for the GDR, where people have become far maturer in political terms, thanks to the pressure they have been under, than we have in the West. The fundamental error of the Germans is that they are all Hegelians – that is to say, idealists. Ideas, ideologies and ideals of some kind or another are meat and drink to them. That was why they didn't see that Hitler was heading straight for war. What they saw were ideas. He used ideas and ideals – the blond nordic Aryan, the pure breed – and the Germans fell for it. The Germans fall for ideas very easily. It is their great strength; and they pay for it with all manner of destruction and loss. It is something we have in common with the Israelis – with the Jews, to be exact. They base their lives on an ideology too. Of course the Zionists that went to Palestine were not doing so for economic reasons: they had an idea – home, back to the land of our fathers. And they're paying for it to this day, bitterly. People say they could think more pragmatically and could get on fine with the Arabs. They *can't*. I understand that perfectly. They have that fanaticism characteristic of peoples for whom religion and politics are one and the same thing. You may object that that wasn't the case in Germany, but I say it was. Under Hitler, it was. National Socialism was an *ersatz* religion. Or take Iran, which is a striking example. Peoples that are governed by an idea and ideology end up having to pay for it, terribly. We Germans are a people of that kind. We have paid – and now (I'm tempted to say: unfortunately) we are reaping a reward again, a very prompt reward. We have become wealthy and bourgeois again too fast. We haven't suffered fully. It is like someone with an illness, or in psychoanalysis: he has to go through the crisis if he's to become perfectly healthy again. If he doesn't, or if he avoids the crisis, the bacillus or neurosis will still be in him. I'm not trying to say that the Fascist elements in today's Germany are greater than in other countries. But the Germans are a highly susceptible people and their minds are easily steamrollered by ideals and big ideas.

MH: You also called the Germans a 'necrophiliac' people when we were talking earlier on.

LR: I'm using the word in Erich Fromm's

86

sense. He distinguishes between necrophiliac and biophiliac people and peoples. Take a people such as the Japanese, for instance: hara-kiri. Peoples like the Japanese are intent on self-sacrifice. They see self-sacrifice as their greatness. You would never get an Italian kamikaze pilot. For the Italians, heroes are idiots. The Italian says: We want to live, we want to dance, eat, and love. The Germans aren't like that. They may not commit hara-kiri, or fly kamikaze missions – though they *did* do that, the Stukkas knew very well they were flying to their deaths on the London raids, but no one talks about that. Love of heroism has its wonderful side, but the Germans pay dearly for it. Is it worth it? Necrophiliac peoples want heroism (which includes the cult of male strength), self-sacrifice, and war as the inevitable consequence. In that sense, we Germans have all the signs of necrophilia. The positive side of it is orderliness, good behaviour and reliability.

MH: In 1968 when you re-read Albee's *Who's Afraid of Virginia Woolf* you noted: 'I find that "private problems" now strike me as old-fashioned.' If I look at your own work in the light of that comment, it's striking that you tend to return to 'public' subjects – though of course they involve individual people and private lives. You seem to see your function as that of a maker of public attitudes, tackling public problems.

LR: One thing I have learnt in a long, full life is that nobody is an individual. There are no individual cells: everything, the whole world, is connected. Once when I was talking to a school class, conversation turned to collective guilt – it was a few years ago and the party were Austrians, trying to pretend it was no concern of theirs. 'But we never...', and so on. So then I had an idea, an idea I've used again at times since then. I said: Hit the table. Now what did you do? 'I hit the table.' No; you set countless molecules in the wood in motion. Do you suppose the movement ceases at the edge of the table? You know enough about physics to know that the waves continue. And where do they stop? Nowhere. Perhaps at the end of the universe. In other words, your individual action affects the whole world. You cannot act in individual isolation, whether it be for good or for evil, Your actions take place in society. You are a creature of society. I well remember how shocked the pupils were. I tried to soothe them by saying: The good you do is felt far and wide, however insignificant the action.

I deliberately live as one human part of the whole of humanity – not as a part of a people or nation. I have always been opposed to nationalism, and still am now, of course, more than ever. Nor am I content with being a European. Nor with being merely a human being. I am only satisfied if I can see myself as a cell in the totality of Creation. I love plants and animals; they are my brothers and sisters. So-called inanimate matter is not inanimate either. We are all one. The experience of that universal oneness is (for me) one of the most beautiful experiences old age has to offer. And of course my social, political and ethical attitudes derive from it.

MH: In that respect you resemble Goethe in old age.

LR [*laughing*]: I'm always happy to be compared to Goethe!

MH: The oneness of things is one of the subjects Goethe is forever returning to in his late poetry.

LR: Every year or so I go back to reading Goethe, and every time I discover him anew. He was the great sage. A very old soul, if you will permit me to put it esoterically. He knew a great deal. Of course it would be gratifying if you were to compare the insight of my old age with Goethe's. But shouldn't it be the goal of every one of us? We should at least long to attain it. A few years ago I came across a phrase in Hegel's Berlin lectures – 'the infinite energy of longing'.

MH: I'd like to ask you about one of your contemporaries, Ernesto Cardenal. You were in Frankfurt when Cardenal was awarded the West German book trade's Peace Prize in 1980, and the question you felt to be central was: How can someone who has been at once a priest and a revolutionary, committing acts of violence, be awarded a *Peace* Prize? You noted in your journal that the crux was whether what was ultimately being aimed at was a condition of peace. Isn't that too much like saying that the end justifies the means?

LR: If I had been Ernesto Cardenal I would not have accepted the prize. He came from a country where people who demonstrated for peace were locked up or prevented from pursuing their professions, and which manufactured arms for wars in Central America. But of course he wanted to draw attention to the problems of his country. I am often asked if I would fight if there were a revolution. I cannot make any easy reply. Nowadays I am against force; but there are times when violence results not in further violence but in peace. When the Allies liberated Germany in 1945, the use of force was our salvation. In Korea, the use of force represented liberation from brutal Japanese dominance. Now, of course, the President of North Korea says: 'I had blood on my hands once, liberating my country, and I shall never use force again.' He said as much to me. As for myself, I am pleased I have never had to face the decision of killing an 'enemy' – that is to say, murdering a human being. But I am not sure how

I would have responded at one time if it had been a question of toppling an evil régime.

MH: It's also a matter of whether the régime is legal and/or legitimate, isn't it?

LR: Which government is ever completely legal?

MH: I'm thinking of your note on Pope Leo XV's encyclical.

LR: Which said that in certain circumstances – if no other alternative remained – a revolution was permissible. Revolutions are always bloody. True revolutions, that is. Anything else is evolution. Or reform. Or whatever you want to call it.

MH: One last question. In *Grenzübergänge* [*Border Crossings*, 1972] you describe a scene in which you ask Martin Buber, 'Herr Buber, what is God in your view?' and he replies: 'God? I love him.' Banal as the scene is, it has a kind of magnificence. How does Luise Rinser see God? Sometimes you see yourself as a single cell in a universe where everything is interconnected, and at other times (frequently) you emphasize life as movement, as a dynamic force, and the name you give to that force is simply 'God'.

LR: One needs a word to express something that cannot be understood. For me – and this is Hegelian again – God is the spirit of the world, the primaeval source of all energy. I studied theology for years, and have 'forgotten' it all, on purpose.

But that Aramaic Jew Yeshua, who we know by the Latinized form of his name, Jesus, is as close to me as a brother. That is why I wrote my novel *Mirjam* [1983] about him. Oddly enough, it was a great success – not only in terms of sales but in terms of the spirit. It prompted a great many people who were looking for religion to think. The book brought me a vast number of readers' letters, from intellectual 'atheists' and from simple seekers and believers. The loveliest letter I got was from an Egyptian Moslem woman, a scholar of German, who wrote that if a Christian believer and a Moslem believer could understand each other at so profound a level it was reason for great hope.

I don't have any new message to offer. Simply this: Love one another and create peace. I do not have any more to say.

NOTES

1   The first and so far only volume of autobiography published by Luise Rinser (1981), covering her youth, the Second World War, and her beginnings as a writer.

2   Ernst Jünger's book was first published in 1929 and immediately withdrawn by the author. A second, radically revised version appeared in 1938. It consists of sixty-odd prose 'capriccios' (Jünger's term) varying in length; the 100-word description of the tiger-lily, projecting fascination with death and narcotic decay onto the flower, is the first of them.

3   'Thomas Mann und der Sozialismus', written in 1947 but unpublished at that time, was recently included in Luise Rinser's *An den Frieden glauben* [Essays on literature, politics and religion, 1944-67], Fischer, 1990.

4   The only one of Luise Rinser's books currently in print in Britain (Penguin paperback) and one of the few to have been translated into English to date, the *Prison Journal* records two months in a women's gaol in winter 1944 when Rinser, following a denunciation for 'defeatist' and anti-Nazi talk, was being held on a charge of treason and expected a death sentence.

5   The terms mean (literally) 'rubble literature' and 'total clearance'; the first is used to describe the literature of the immediate post-'45 years, written in and about the bombed towns and cities of Germany, while the second refers rather more broadly to the sense that everything had been wiped out and that it was necessary (in literature too) to start again from scratch.

6   In fact 'Leben auf dem hohen Seil' was published in the *Neue Zeitung* (Munich), 11 October 1950.

The interview was conducted in Cologne on 21 November 1989.